Do Something Useful

Siam

Illustrator Polly Thompson

Edward Gaskell *publishers*
DEVON

First published 2008
Edward Gaskell *publishers*
Old Sawmill
East-the-Water
Bideford
Devon
EX39 3DX

isbn   (10) 1-898546 -95 9
           (13) 978 -1898546 - 95 -5

© siam
© illustrations Polly Thompson

Do Something Useful

Siam

Illustrator Polly Thompson

All rights reserved. No part of this publication may be reproduced, stored in a retrieval system, or transmitted in any form by any means electronic, mechanical, photocopying, scanning, recording or otherwise, without the prior written permission of the publishers.

Typeset, printed and bound by
Lazarus Press
Caddsdown Business Park
Bideford
Devon
EX39 3DX
WWW.LAZARUSPRESS.COM

Dedicated to

our respective children and grandchildren

Siam

Siam, erstwhile Patricia Churchill, evicted convent girl and maverick, was brought up Edwardianly on ponies, boats, old Irish silver and chess, until she betook herself off to an alternative life in the Sudan for 25 years. There she raised her own beloved family before coming back to settle hermit-like in the Welsh hills, coming full circle, a celebrating elder, globe trotting between her many grand-children. She finds great delight in lolling in hammocks and on farm gates as of youthful yore, chewing her perennial existential cud and 'happily running out of words'.

Siam's work is not about answers. This selection of her writings includes some of her earlier collaborations with Polly and conveys something of the visionary and shamanic quality of her story-telling; she feels that the sensual nature of Polly's artistic assurance adds a tantalizing visual perspective to her own quixotic images and mindscapes.

Polly

Having lived, worked, and exhibited in many countries including Sudan, Polly now lives in Appledore. She has a great affinity with the sea and rivers and loves swimming, sailing, rowing and walking by the sea. A major part of her work as an artist is based on the theme of Water. She also enjoys working on Portraits and Landscapes. The illustrations for Siam's writings are viewed as expressions of mutual inspiration. She has also undertaken commissions to do archaeological and botanical illustrations. She has held many solo exhibitions both overseas and in UK, three at the specific invitation of British Council. Her work is in collections all over the world.

Polly studied at Canterbury and Bristol College of Art specialising in Fine Art as her main subject and Hand Printed and Woven textiles as additional. She has a Diploma in Education from London University and a Masters in Anthropology and Archaeology from Cambridge.

Contents

Babies Are Big   06

That Was the Beginning of That   09

Cat   12

Any Spot Will Do For Me   21

Do Something Useful   24

Isn't it a Fact   26

Nothing Like   29

Gorilla   32

Hermit   34

Mind Weavers   46

The Gentleman from Turkestan   48

The Wind In My Treetops   50

Purple Swans   53

Comforter of Time Passing   56

Father Dear   58

Two Pound Cut   59

Of Adam, of Eve   62

Conker Girl   68

Whose Who   70

H$_2$O   74

Child of Straw   76

BABIES ARE BIG

Baby is big
big business:
alien creature supreme
in its cuckoo nest
an evolutionary time-bomb
in the guise of this raw, bare blob
whom no-one could suspect of subversive intent.

Baby is diddums
mummy's sweet apple
fat in her eye, so innocent
all of the planet oogles, besotted
triggered by each snuffle
and conditioned not to see
how *huge* this foreign body is
precipitously plonked from galactic otherwheres
into the captive lap of stunned progenitors
who believe this miracle was consciously planned
- via loins and bank - every hair just *so*.

But they come in hoards around the clock
each one an extra-terrestrial squatter
dumb and penniless
invaders claiming natal rights
of inheritance, of territory, of precedence.

Where is your ID kiddo?
twiddling your toes, guileless
you immigrant angel
seeded so the natives do not see how you slip in
or even question.

Baby is *not*
a (re)-production line cog
a replacement gimmick
no mere begin-er without a strategy.
It is the ultimate agenda, hidden
by its simple transparency.
Oh! babies are big.

THAT WAS THE BEGINNING OF THAT

Alright! build me an ark
and I will find a nubile pair of every kind
- excepting *man,* who doesn't count
being of no survival value whatsoever.

Even I, the oracle
will not ride that saving boat
nor my legal next of kin
but will sling it off fully packed and programmed
and stay behind for the collective free-for-all regatta
ensured for all
all holds barred.

Certainly, the safely reflex apes
and predictably murderous doves
will manage better.

Then up spake the Lord

No you won't, oh ninny-witted fool!
that's too idiotic for words.
You must arrange at least:
one helmsman
one compass reader
one psychologist
one signal-man
one captain
one midwife
one astronomer
one fish-wife
one actress
one game-warden
one cook
one accountant
for crew.

Who on earth do you think
will feed the snakes and make the tea?
- not to mention co-ordinate post-deluvial re-allocations
oh my! oh me!
The day I created that man-thing!
"in my image", my foot!
Brains?
Phooey! they must have fallen out
when that silly first lady fell down.

So thus chastised
I sent out a prime-time advert for said jobs
plus, taking the hint
for an ecologist, medicine-person, engineer
zen master, dentist etc
and due to the rampant unemployment in those days
it was no time before the required personnel
were interviewed, vaccinated, insured
and set to work.

Even I.
As the reporter, the resident scribe
(letter-writer, contract-ratifier
mouthpiece, odd-jobs man, go-between)
to translate reports into acceptably far-fetched legends
for the prime benefit of posterity
- who, actually
prefer not to benefit from *any*thing
let alone historical precedents or scientific probabilities
- analogies/auguries/fairy-tales et al.

And so, without more ado
womph!
down fell the waters from Above
up billowed the briny from Below
duly submerging
every tide-mark, false-hope, telegraph-pole
and weather satellite:
gravitational vortices
polar melts
crustal subsidences
axial wobbles
and electronic brainstorms
being the order of the day
for those of a technical turn of mind.

And, as you may imagine
that was the beginning of That!

CAT

There was once upon ago, an old woman who lived all alone in a hut on the edge of a forest. Those were the days of witches and werewolves, giants and goblins, but she wasn't afraid of anything like that.

Though it must be said that the villagers were afraid of *her*; in fact they were afraid of *anything* they could not control. Which was more or less *everything*. She grew herbs and vegetables, keeping a goat for milk and cheese and a cat for company.

Now one day, she sat carding the wool scraps she had gathered from the brambles, the pale winter sun hanging in the bare branches of late afternoon, when the cat sprung up from his sleep and staring her straight in the eye said: *There is a visitor outside dear, you'd better invite him in.*

The old woman of course, had not heard a sound, but the creak and the hiss of the wind soughing in the conifers and far away the somnolent sound of the waterfall. She rose, and opening the door went outside, peering this way and that in the gathering dusk. At first she not could make out anything but the blurred, bluish shapes of the bushes and boulders at the edge of the clearing. Then, a tiny movement caught her eye and she became aware of a figure standing motionless among the shadows, poised and sere as a reed, watching her. Without hesitation she called out,

Welcome stranger! Come and take bread with me! Have no fear!

So he came forward towards her, with the last rays of daylight illuminating the rim of his silhouette from behind, like the halo of an eclipse. He followed her into the hut, seating himself on the bench to which she ushered him. She then set about raking the ashes, adding a log to the embers, poking it so that it spat and sizzled, seeping coils of thick, resinous smoke into every cranny and rafter of the little dwelling. She was perfectly accustomed to the companionable intimacies of silence so she felt no need to bandy words about.

But as she shredded rosemary into the broth and slung the quavering rush lantern from a beam, she noticed that her guest was of a physiognomy completely different from anything she'd ever heard of or seen. He was extremely etiolated, and as she focussed through the smoky gloom she realised his skin was a silvery, mauve colour, while his hair was blue black, like the mantle of deadest night. As she met his quizzical eyes the shock of their gold and amber hue seemed to pour a torrent of flame into her own.

She was not the sort to feed on or foster fear, but the strangeness overwhelmed her. Seating herself abruptly she said, *I think you come from distant lands traveller?*

"A long, <u>long</u> way off, yes," he replied. The cat meanwhile was wreathing round his ankles, rumbling deeply.

But I had been led to believe that strange tongues were spoken over the wide waters and the snow hills. Yet you speak our dialect as well as Hanroff the Letter man himself. . .

"My home is farther away than that, my good friend. There, we have no problem with communication."

Which explained nothing! Nevertheless it provided fuel for reflection. Later that evening the traveller addressed her saying, " You lead a hard life it would seem, and a solitary one, my honourable hostess?"

Oh, no, indeed, she replied. *I lead a full and fruitful life; my cat, he is my family and friend. We are busy, according to the seasons, but with leisure enough to share their moods, breathe the twilight in the sky and find here,* gesturing towards the timbered walls, *shelter from the rain. Nor are we bothered by the creatures that prey on the villagers: the Trolls that raid the flocks and steal the children, the Valkyries setting the thatches on fire, the rapacious bands of man, violating, crushing, grabbing. The things of darkness find no sport here - an old woman without ambitions or dreads. What could they find to feast on in* me? *As for cat!*

It is precisely the matter of these "creatures" you mention, that brings me to these parts. Perhaps you could tell me more?" asked the guest.

Well, there's not much to it sir, she answered. *All I know is that in the populated areas there is always the risk - and therefore I suppose the presence, of some monster's depredations. No one is safe, they are all always afraid. I myself had to run away from my home simply because I could not share their terror and therefore was considered a bad omen.*

"And why was that, may I ask" interrupted the other, "weren't you at risk too?"

Well, when I was a child, apparently, a werewolf was seen to run away *from me. I remember it clearly! This was because I thought he was a friendly dog! I daresay if I'd realised what it really was I would have provided it with the fear it needed!* and she chuckled whimsically remembering; *after that I was regarded as being possessed by some evil spirit, and if I had not run away, I would surely have met one of the grizzly 'ends' my people are so ingenious at concocting.*

The old woman lapsed into silence, and the only sound was the purring of the cat, draped liquidly over the visitors lap, and the black night whispering around the corners of the hut.

After a while the man spoke again. "You see, some entity/energy that never should have had any access to this world at all, is finding a breach, a way in. I am come to make a preliminary report. Something of this nature - introduction of a totally aberrant factor, against which neither the ecosystem nor its species have built up any antibodies or resistance - has to be dealt with, with great precision, if the corrective measures aren't going to put us back to square one."

The old woman was evidently finding difficulty following this. *Some sort of demon giant or chimera, you mean? A new kind of vampire parasite? But I know, we know that* all *of them live on fear, and therefore what the cure is. I don't know what you mean by 'corrective measures', if not that.*

"You, my respected friend, are looking at this in a personal, individual sense. Now can you visualize a communal sort of monster or disease? In which no amount of separate fearlessness would be of the least account. Compare it with the plague. An infectious conduit that breeds, according to its nature (as all things will) more of the same stuff".

If that's the case, I don't see what you or anyone *could do,* objected the woman.

"Well, there are some things that can be done; but not by me or you individually certainly. Yet in a funny way, each *you* and each *me* are vital, in the sense that we can <u>combine</u> our efforts, intentions, energies etc. so that altogether they amount to more than the sum of their separate parts. Do you follow? Cat for example is certainly more than his component parts of whiskers, entrails fur, purpose etc."

When I scrape flint on flint it makes. . .fire! That's it isn't it?

"Precisely" said the man, blinking in surprise.

So?

"Well the least drastic measure would be the introduction of a new belief system, or renovation of an old one. Imagine say, a loud Trumpet or a Chariot coming out of the sky; or a Voice delivering some kind of Message; or that Oracles, Alpha graded individuals should produce inspired instructions in the line of *the Necessity demands, The King of the world declares* or *Big Chief is angry if you do this or that.* Add a few startling phrases and melodramatic 'signs', hey presto, there's a new religion for you.

If the situation has deteriorated beyond such simple remedies, the required amendment can often be brought about by minor and localised geographical upheavals, for example a timely flood or drought. However it often proves that such corrective surgery is only of short term and superficial influence.

In more extreme cases it involves a wider scale employment of natural disasters but of <u>global</u> proportions. The purpose always being, after shock therapy fail, to dispose of as much of the aberrant species as possible, while maintaining a viable gene pool for future re-populating - and of course adequate provision for the survival of animal and plant genera. Too extreme measures could reduce the place to a rubble heap like your moon.

Even among my own people there is a growing party of those who would prefer the most radical option. We however are not so pessimistic - otherwise I would not be here! Nevertheless, it is apparent that severe course corrections <u>are</u> required. . ."

Suddenly the man stopped his discourse. He realised the old woman had nodded off to sleep and he had been lecturing the cat - who he knew had no need of such!

"Fool!" he addressed himself, laughing. Then with great gentleness he tucked a rough-woven rug round her and tipping sozzled puss into her lap, he tip-toed out into the night and was never seen again.

* * * * * * * * * * * *

Now we jump ahead a good few years and we stop by the same spot we left off. But what is this? There indeed is a kind of dwelling and if there wasn't an ancient crone with an aged cat there, we would never have believed this was the same place. Where forests and horizons of wooded hills had stretched in all directions, it was now a bleak sulphur laden wilderness, of lava, ash and boulder; while a harsh grey sea roared and rolled where once there was a waterfall. A few gulls planed on the raw edges of the air; apart from that and the old woman, there was no visible sign of life. In fact tremors and currents ran through the ground and a low subterranean growl was detectable, from deep under the earth. The sky was screened by lowering banks of cloud shot through by a lurid glow on the horizon.

Then there was another movement. From round the cliff edge came a small boy, clutching a fistful of what seemed to be seaweed and molluscs. He went over to the old woman, displaying his trophies for her inspection. Cat rose and wrapped his tail round his bony shins, rasping the boy's dirty cheek with his candy-floss tongue as he squatted there on the ground.

I will tell you about the forest began the old woman.
In those days the trees were towering into the sky like this, extending her withered old arm in a gesture embracing the high heavens.
The squirrels would make nests in the branches and chase one another up and down in sheer joie de vivre. Over there where the new waters tip over the end of the world, there used to be snow hills; and the sky was blue, blue as you never knew. . . on and on she rambled, while the lad, who had heard it all a hundred times, wondered at these fantastic and unlikely tales.
"Still" he told himself, "it does no harm, it keeps her happy; and it's not a bad *idea* after all."
Then he'd laugh at himself for being so foolish as to be susceptible to such fantasies.
Trees, huh! Up to the sky! He knew that all he could validly go by was what he *knew*. And he knew perfectly well that the world was all rock and yellow fumes and belching noises and slimey sea-weed. Yet also there was Her and Cat. So he was perfectly content. Even, on occasions, he would indulge in concocting such fanciful stories for his own entertainment: "Once upon ago there were these kinds of gigantic seaweed that grew up and up into the clouds. . . ." And then he would tumble Cat over onto her back and tickle her tummy, saying - "Really Cat, what next? I'll be believing there <u>were</u> flowers and girls and singing animals once!"

One afternoon in this infinity of indeterminate afternoons, the boy came leaping and calling across the sharp rocks, waving in his hand a streamer of green.
"Look! Look!" he shouted.
The old lady fingered the lacy scrap, while the boy impatiently asked "What is it? What <u>is</u> it?"
A vine or a creeper, child, she replied. *One of those things I told you about.*
His mouth fell open and he turned the greeny thing over, smelled it, textured it;
"but it was coming out of the rock, I had to pull it out" he went on.

So next time the old woman proposed yet another of her extraordinary tales, the boy was a degree less incredulous:

I will tell you: once this giant purple man, the colour of the sea when it's angry, came to me; oh, he came from far across the hills; he said and he spoke of all the fiends and demons and he smiled with eyes made of fire. A shudder of horrible delight went down the boy's spine, just imagine it! he thought.

It was then that I had a dream, she continued,

The dream that I told you about, in which I was shown where I would find you! Well I did, didn't I! she asserted.

That dream was warning me that the mountains would fall down and the sea upturn, that a dragon would come out of the sky and whip the rocks to dust with his tail, grind the trees to pulp. That the Fire Monster in the pits under the mountain roots would break loose and devour everything."

She paused, musing over those almost unbelievable happenings. She herself almost accepted that it was all some dream. . . the trees, the birds, the long scented grasses - surely, as the boy said, she *did* dream it all?! So what then was that dream within a dream? Something to do with cleaning up a mess and making a new start? And what did the stranger have to do with it? Didn't he make some mention of earthquakes, tidal waves - or was that <u>the</u> dream? Or 'measures'? 'Risks?' 'Guardianships'? Oh dear, it was so confusing!

Yet there was one thing for sure. Bestirring herself from her musings she spoke:

That green thing, boy, that is what matters. One day, if you guard it right, it will sprout all those magics I told you about: water lilies, fruits, flowers, sunbeams, squirrels. . .

"Even trees?"
Yes, even trees!

ANY SPOT WILL DO FOR ME

There was, believe it or not, this man
sitting in his usual spot
(latitude 22°, Longitude 55°, 19.22 GMT)
It was a cell by all accounts, though he himself considered it not:
My cell is myself, he'd remind the visiting cockroaches
and Jehovah's Witnesses;
Any spacetime spot is OK by me.

"But, poor thing!" wailed the media
and consequently, Public Opinion
"even if he doesn't appreciate his dilemma
we (of the sensitive consciences) do".
And so on.

19.22 wasn't visiting time
and due to the equinox, it was sunset
a stray wisp of reputedly virginal moon doing its siren act.
But he was a Scorpio
so the moon made no headway with him.
He just sat there in his study with the cat on his knee.

After a while
He became aware of someone sitting in the chair opposite him.
Heaven knows (perhaps it did!) how long she'd been there
- it could have been *years*.
It was just a matter of focusing.
Well, there must be some message/reason/chore, he thought.
She's not going to go to all this bother, just to sit there.
With which thought, he coughed, *Ahem*!
and offered the traditional welcome
suggesting a cup of tea.

Is there…I mean, would you….do you care to…?
"Not at all, my friend;
my motive, being Zenish, precedes its cause
and hence is pointless!"
So there was no need for him to know that
at 20.00hrs that same evening
a good sized lump of anti-matter was due to arrive
and - such was the plan - somewhat rearrange the planetary jigsaw.
This was not predicted by the astronomers and physicists
(theory being considered no more than hypothetical
not to mention relative)
and no one, naturally, believed any *un*-natural word the prophets said.
But - have you got there before me, O best beloved? -
this man was intended to survive.
Genetically.

So, looking at her watch, the visitor suggested, to pass the time
that it might be pleasant and fruitful, to make love.
You see, it wasn't only the Grecian gods
who thought eugenically like that.
Looking intently at her, he realised
yes, he could!
So forthwith, luxuriantly and without haste or hesitation
They *did*.

By the time the lump arrived
the good lady (angel, by some accounts)
had removed herself and her precious load
and all went roughly as expected
give or take a bent spoke or two
due to predictably malicious spanners.

On a spot, say Latitude 55°, Longitude 22°
on a volcanic atoll in the middle of a brand-new sea
a child sat, playing with the molluscs and mutant dolphins
and he was thinking:
Now, if I take this spare, bendy rib and mould it just so
I don't see why I can't construct a more interesting companion
than these - albeit dear - crustaceans et al.
Or someone could do it for me.
Apart from that wrinkle in the dunlopillow
any spot will do for me. . .

DO SOMETHING USEFUL

Once there was
this old man, so old his Old Man's Beard
was tattered as Time
with the grief and joy of knowing.

It was all long, bent grass in that distant land
mile upon mile of waving green
naked against the shape of the sky.
Somewhere in that silvery, shifting sea
with the wind crying and calling in its flying mane
was the old man's home.

He used to use his time - not spend it
running across those wide plains
his wild beard streaming in the wind-honed green
twirling his arms like windmills.

His lady wife
who I have not mentioned so far
because she rather spoils the poetry
disapproved of all that grass
and the way her husband gambolled about like a spring-daft colt
shouting and prancing on the specs of shining air.

"Be your age!
Do something useful" she would chide
as she busied herself with her gadgets and precise technology.

But he continued to run barefoot through the grasslands
the sun lolling between silky dawns and peach-dusks
while moons rose and fell
- tapers and melons slung among the starlight
and he would bring back
wild mint and honey-comb for tea.

ISN'T IT A FACT?

I hadn't gone far, not very
down the sequential road
when I came across - as certainly as any chance -
this strange, unstranger man
mending a boot in the ditch.

Isn't it a fact
that one tends to meet people while travelling
as if one *should*?!
It is mostly a disaster
in other words, cosmically essential.
This was.

Child of sorrow and sagacity, hi there! said he, waving his boot.
What? said I. *What for?*
(thinking churlishness might undo unlove).

Daughter of contempt and devastating cheer, hello! he amended.
He was nothing if not sure, in his ageless age.
OK ancient one! I snapped.
I'll do it!
Give me the bootlace!
He was without fingers. A leper, you see.

Certainly not, infant of perdition.
I have my self-respect to respect.
My free desolation.
My own inalienable right to pain.

Which was uncalled for as I knew it.
But then, he only *said* it because I did!

Alright, as you wish.
But don't think I mind.
Deciding to unpack for the night.

Care for a game of chess, then?
So for several spokes of time we played the master game
without a further word but how the eyes own terror speaks
- while the rain filtered into necks and nerves
into packed-lunches and resistances;
there being no trees, umbrellas, lighthouses, or bus shelters around
- only the road and sky, brimming with H^2O and space.

By this time, the King and Queen had met their match
fell in love, wham! and check-mated
it was no news being strangers, with no-thing in between.

Then a virus
(the macrocosmic monster, the microcosmic keeper of the Law)
got the better of his chemistry in the classic shape of pneumococci.
So I dug a trench
and with great solemnity buried him
placing the chessmen and boot
in the mud, to mark the spot
- for the benefit of posterity's relic-mongers.

Before he departed
Light-burdened and god-sped
with only his karmic seed to bear
(and leaving me with the weighty effects)
he gave me a wink and said
O creature of promiscuous silences
call him Emmanuel!

NOTHING LIKE

Once there were two tramps
who followed the lanes, byways and seasons of urbania
living like the lilies of the fields
on the maggoty fruit of affluence and conscientious objection.
The backdoor of the Savoy, the welfare of plenty
and even the sharing of privation and stupidity
their scapegoat and wherewithal
- discreetly carried out by post.

It was a rewarding existence, compared with that
of their unmotivated and alienated forebears
who had eeked out an unbalanced diet and psychotic withdrawal
in the ditches and debris of the countryside
- supposedly cram full of pastoral verse and idyllic sentiment
but, actually, which consisted of muck and drizzle
nettles, draughts and soggy haystacks
as well as east winds, mouldy turnips, landlords, lice
and measly men;
or rather, their mean-fisted mates
those guardians of the hearth and purse:
paragons of uncharity - very pretty!
Well, one day, they were passing the time
- or being passed by - come to think of it
connecting the relay system of a holographic phone
to a transmitter set
quite harmlessly there,
minding their own business in the empty sewer
when along came a vizor'd constable with a detector
on the lookout, so it turned out
for a stolen barrel of industrial cobalt.

If it's not you, Gutherington-Foss! he exclaimed.
What ho! replied G.F. whose old man
had made a fortune on counterfeit lunar rock samples
doing nicely, I see.
Which in fact, he did not
but they had been to the same pre-prep school
so there were certain formalities to observe.

Suddenly, there was a loud crash
and the sound of panicing feet.
Faggots and micro-chips, it must be the RATS!
cried the policeman
and lowering his infra-red goggles
he bolted off down the tunnel
without so much as a Masonic Sign by way of farewell.

And indeed, there emerged, running wildly
a crowd of women with prams and shopping trolleys
high on the neap tide of X plus terror.
On coming to the intersection, with one accord
they dived down the tunnel in which the tramps were working
and raced past on pure octane adrenalin
with the pig-sized rats hot on their high heels…

Nothing like a bit of real fear
to stimulate the communal psyche
remarked GF.
Nothing like! agreed his mate.

GORILLA

I met a hairy gorilla in the sky-washed street
He was black and shambly like a Doubt.

I tapped his shoulder kindly
And, when the flea-cloud had settled
He turned his stunted, marble eyes
And through his railing teeth:
I beg your pardon Madam?
Then, hitching up his saggy hide
Sidled into a jet-set bar
And ordered Korsakoff's Scheherazade.

I clambered to my high perch stool
And steered his slipping cranium
Into my line of sight: *are you from these parts?*
The fidgety silence of convention made me ask.

But his impervious, one-dimensional eyes
Got hooked on someone at the door
And, to my surprise
His only answer was a grunt.

Then, putting down a gentlemanly tip
From behind his rubber-mould ear
And, in his hurry, going on all fours
He went across to her
Extending his rack-fractured paw.

And I was left to wonder how I'd aged.

HERMIT THE WOLF

Now, once upon a time there was a big wolfish wolf. No doubt about it, he was! I won't call him bad just because he was a **wolf** and liable to steal lambs, kids and sheepskin coats off washing lines - and gobble them up; for that was, after all, the nature of his nature and it would hardly be appropriate for him to be, let alone look like, say, a reindeer, a Pekinese puppy or a wallaby or something, would it? So, indeed, there he most definitely was, very wolfy for sure and now begins my tale…or do I mean his?! - which was very long and ratty, among other things. . .

One day, when the birds were singing in the blackthorn, the sky was as blue as my Morning Glories and the Persil-bright washing was flapping merrily in the cottage gardens, while hazy smoke drifted across the tree-tops from the local oil refinery, (etc) round the corner came Hermit Wolf trundling the littlest wolfling in its pram. Super-Jo, such was he called, was teething madly, so was practicing gnawing on an antique ptero-dactyl bone-rattle with his brand-new gnashers. He just gnashed it up like a biscuit, then proceeded in chain-saw style, to gnaw along the edge of the pram, spitting out the bits with venom and accuracy into the faces of the passing ducks, donkeys and old age pensioners. Hermit, observing these dear little wolfish antics, commended the babe, saying:
A chip off the old block, the little lamb! and <u>*That's the way!*</u> *Get 'em where it hurts, eh!*

Thus they continued down the High Street, dispensing this routine and traditional, daily quota of devasta-tion and dismay. This had been going on for literally **ages** - ages before the last Ice Age even. So the people were fairly adapted, conditioned and accustomed to this state of affairs and in this manner the Natural Order kept its balances and everything appeared hunky dory. It might have gone on like this until kingdom come if Super-Jo hadn't finally over-reached himself - which is called *hubris* - by catching the Mayor's wife a bulls-eye in the back-side with a sharp segment of enamel pram handle. This upset the extant order of nature, being the last straw that bent the camel's hump, so at last public wrath rose like a phoenix (one of those rare species of flying fish, which abounded in those parts) culminating in a Secret Conclave in which it was resolved:
What we'll do is **kidnap** *the little beast*
announced Ms Cow, long cobwebs of dribble dangling from her mushy blue nose.
That will give wolf a real fright and we can wallop Super-Jo within an inch of his wolvine life!

But

interrupted Mr. Haggle-Back, the village scribe, who also served as policeman, gravedigger and innkeeper all in one

I suggest it would be wiser to kidnap wolf himself; who gives a bat's tooth for a piffling brat? What we need to do is get the master-mind himself. . .

And <u>then</u> what? Liquidate him? On what grounds? Isn't he always technically on the right side of, well, er at least the judge and the traffic lights?

someone added.

Well, we could have him certified and locked up. Then we could have his brood safely interned in the Brain-washing clinic for a while

suggested Miss Warp, the local primary school Principle.

Ho! You're joking!

snorted Jemimah Spoon, the resident Jehovah's Witness, who simply loathed Miss Warp on account of her warts,

Who do you reckon is willing to sign the certificate? Doctor Pot? When you know perfectly well that he and Hermit are paw-in-hand, thick as thistles; they even play Canasta together and share their subscription to Look Forward to Yesterday.

There was a general shuffling and huffling of agreement. Everyone knew that Doctor Pot was not to be relied upon - though he certainly was brilliant at diagnosing measles and opening Bazaars. There was a chorus of hums, sighs and rustlings of feet, claws, whiskers, tails, feathers and trunks. The *trunk* belonged to Eggy the Elephant who was absent-mindedly hoovering up fallen peanuts, screws and key-rings; this was an automatic habit with him as he ran a lucrative vacuum and dry-cleaning business in the area. But it wasn't very auspicious for the prospects of his appendix - especially as he'd had it removed years ago.

At last, Ms Cow came up with what must be instantly recognized as a stroke of *genius* - which is a rare commodity called common sense.

What we must do is out-wit them!

she bellowed like a bull, in her excitement.

*We must stop playing <u>their</u> game; we must stop rising to the bait **they** provide us with!*

She paused, breathing lustily, waving a DIY manual on Kung-Fu over her, um, horns. By now everyone was listening, so she went on:

*Look! Don't they **mean** to be anti-social, disruptive?*

Yeah! Yeah!

Everyone shouted.

Isn't it their policy? Don't they do it on purpose? As a <u>principle</u> even?
she continued.

Yeah! Oh yeah!

Even though they pretend they don't, they do - don't they!?

Yeah! Yeah!
stamping their feet in assorted rhythm.

So what does this <u>mean?</u> You, Oggleworth! What do you think it means?
Poor Oggleworth, who was the only intellectual in the University, got such a fright that he just blubbered and blathered and then ran out of the room so precipitately that he went head over heels over the balcony rail. Ten seconds later (for they were on the 7th Floor) they heard a loud splash as he landed in the duck-pond.

Poor thing!
Everyone murmured.
Now what would he do? He'll be all wet and his mother is a Tartar; she won't stand for wet bibs, socks or mortar boards. Then they remembered that she had gone for the week-end to stay with her sister in the Caucasus; so they heaved a sigh of relief and returned their attentions to Chair-Lady Cow.

With a toss of her horns (of which she was very proud and never missed the opportunity to throw them, plus her own weight, around - if she got the chance) she dismissed the Oggleworth interlude and continued to explain:
*What this **means**, comrades and everyone else, is this: that, for some strange reason, the wolf-nature lives on, nay! <u>thrives on</u> the resistance that WE give them. They need and want the precise responses and reactions that we so bovine-ly - um! sheepishly, oh sorry! I meant <u>moronically</u> (that's the word!) provide. So? So, if we are to be canny and out-wit them, we must **not** offer them what they want. Therefore, we must **not** allow ourselves to become angry, anxious, outraged, upset!*

By now everyone was listening open-mouthed, expressions of shock, disbelief, intrigue and dawning com-prehensions flitting from face to face. After a ruminative pause, someone spoke up:
*And **then** what, Ms Cow?*
Then
she pronounced grandly

Then! *You just wait! You will have the surprise of your lives! You'll witness a change in the wolf behavior that will signify the end to all our strife and sorrow.*

That was a claim and a half! Then, getting into higher gear, girding her loins - milk-bags, I mean - she went on:
Believe me, the longed for New Kingdom is nigh! The Ideal State, the Utopia of our dreams, Eden re-found. All we have to do is suffer in silence, adhere to the tenets of non-violence and hey presto, Snaggletooth's your uncle!

For how long must we thus suffer?
queried some faint-hearted soul.

Who cares!
bellowed Ms Cow, away on her high horse:
What does it matter how long and how many lives it costs, or how many minds are cracked, hearts broken? Doesn't there have to be a price for everything? And aren't we going to rid ourselves of this canker, this virus, the snake in our midst. . .
and so on and so forth.

At last, even the humans present, came round to see the implications of this undertaking. Why! It might even prove a short cut to Paradise, into the bargain! So, forthwith, this program was agreed upon and put into action.

When Hetty Wolf stole an old lady's ermine stole, she was congratulated on how pretty she looked.

Hermit, *en route* for a pint with the Doc, during his pre-breakfast jog, lifted a neat little petrol-run grass-mower from the Gaggle's front lawn. He was forthwith presented with the key and a spare can of brake fluid in case it squeaked.

Tiddles stuffed Eggy's nose with a wad of bubble-gum and was sent a Valentine card by way of thanks, signed Eggy. Thereupon, Super-Jo, the eldest, not to be outdone, excelled even himself by super-gluing all the super-market trolleys together - which included the Superintendent's hand. He was publicly commended for his initiative by the Manager, while the Superintendent remarked that this hitch had actually been in his favour as he had missed week-end washing-up duty, not to mention, the All-in-Wrestling which he hated.

At this rate spectacular results should not take long in appearing. Nor did they!

Firstly, the wolf family escalated their activities, taking more drastic measure so that their erstwhile delin-quencies began to verge upon organized crime. Though they took care that it wasn't the sort that could be caught.

Hermit hijacked the school bus, which was the village mascot as well and was used on all public holidays for outings, picnics, cross-country treks etc. It was found later, mysteriously jammed in the shaft of the plutonium mine down the hill. A newspaper article praised the high heavens for having spared the commu-nity from that decrepit death-trap of a bus.

Hetty wolf *borrowed* Finnigan, the only child and heir of Count Battenbottle, right from under the nose of his nanny, as she was playing the trombone, to lull him to sleep. Years later, she explained to the Press that she had mistaken Mrs Wolf for Finnigan's mother, who, it was true, had a strong resemblance to Red Riding Hood's gran - they even had the same Marks and Spencer star-wars outfits and wore identical tinted con-tact lenses; so, how was she supposed to have been able to tell the difference? she protested. Identikit pho-tos of Hetty, alongside poly-photos of Finnigan as a second year naval cadet (a time-warp being involved) were plastered all over the place, captioned: *Heroine saves the day*! *Elopes with fairy princess!* This was fol-lowed by florid accounts of a hidden romance and mention of a blank cheque presented by the grateful par-ents. Even Hermit squirmed!

Meanwhile, Tiddles and Super-Jo had not been at a loss for what to do. Super-Jo's "tiny tot chemistry set for beginners" enabled him to blow a gaping hole in the outer wall of the community nuclear reactor. Ofcourse, he was out on a school trip that day. The villagers arranged a disarmament rally in which the environmental activist's subversion of that cess-pit of iniquity was loudly acclaimed and circulated via pam-phlets and street-corner gossip. As for Tiddles' share in these goings-on, he succeeded in stuffing the whole length of the Fire-engine's hose with seaweed and jelly-fish.

So far so good! And you may have noticed how the community was getting into the spirit of it all and becoming quite adept, ingenious and fear-less in the process.

Then, at last, the Wolf family succumbed!
But was that the happy ending of the affair? Had indeed a new age dawned? And if this was so, from a soci-ological point of view, might people be interested to know what kind of job Hermit took up? What sort of training did Super-Jo respond to? Did Hetty contribute constructively to the Whist Drive, the Women's Institute, the Philanthropist's Reserve? How much integration was there?

Well, Hermit became a technician in the Astronomical Observatory and, in fact, he was one of the leading figures to divert Halley's Comet from a crash landing on the Moon. He was even congratulated in the local gazette and awarded a medal. While the rest of his brood took up and became constructive members of the society in various worthy ways. But, as for whether this is the end of the story, NO, not by a long chalk! In fact, it is only the half-way mark, the ice-cream and pepsi interval.

For after a while of this idyllic existence, all the inhabitants began to suffer from some mysterious malaise. They started dropping dead as they walked down to the Post Office. They forgot to feed their babies. They lost interest even in the TV advertisements. Doctor Pot was at his wits-end because, at Medical School, he had never been taught about a fatal dis-ease called Boredom. He bought in a team of experts and they diagnosed a variety of unlikely conditions such as Hypnotic Suggestion from malignant Extra-terrestrials, or an epidemic of contagious Depression - all to no avail.

At which point, the stalwart character of Ms Cow came to the fore. A latent capacity for tyranny and a taste for amassing gold bullion in Swiss banks, stood her in good stead. Before you could say Snaggletooth's your Uncle, she established herself as the resident self-appointed despot and without more ado, set about restabilising (so she claimed) no less than the entire (local) eco-system. She toured the slums and garden estates in her armoured and cocktail-cabineted cattle truck, proclaiming from the loud-speaker that if so much as one more citizen dropped dead again, there would be immediate reprisals. Her shock troopers patrolled the streets with walkie-talkies bleeping, day and night, bayonets at the ready. All five of them.

Thus began the famous Rule of Terror. Mrs Cow, now called MS Cow held the society by its throat with an iron hand - or Hoof. All and any detainees were mercilessly interrogated (she called it *Interview*, to the RSPCA Reps) by herself personally and then plunged into dungeons to rot in manacles with only rats and toads for company. Things got to such a pass that in the end there was hardly anyone left to staff the military Academy, not to mention the Brewery and the Palace Guard.

When this had gone on for long enough and with the Sea-side season approaching, it became apparent to the survivors above ground that no external aid was forthcoming; so they called a top secret meeting in Ye Olde Tea-shop, disguised as American tourists.

After long discussions and arguments they at least came to agree that *something* had to be done. (maybe, in truth, it did not matter **what!**) So, why not have an Election? Madame Frou Frou became quite eloquent; she was ever one for equal representation of the sexes, long as they weren't female - especially as her job title was FCS (Female Chauvinist Sow). She undertook to umpire the Elections and safeguard the rights of, um, well, the entire mammalian creation, actually. A somewhat ambitious undertaking, perhaps! Ah! But one shouldn't sneer at spiritedness; goodness knows, by now they all knew full well what the *lack* of that commodity entailed.

So the options for the Elections were as follows:
1 Yes
2 No
3 Maybe
4 I don't know.
Those standing for office, included Ms Cow, who, being incorrigible, had come along to the Meeting to spy on it. Also, Super-Jo and Ermintrude the Lamb. By the time the voting booths were closed and the results added up, they were found to be as follows: 3 No. 3 Yes. 703, I don't know. Which wasn't very helpful. These must have been a lazy people, concluded Madame Frou Frou. And, come to think of it - she thought to herself - where on earth are they all? She'd forgotten about the dungeons. So the next step, at the next secret meeting was a vote of No Confidence. This was unanimous, minas one. The one being, you might guess, Ms Cow.

By now they were all accomplished actors and could imitate people daintily eating scones and tea quite easily, which, in the circumstances, proved quite an advantage!

However, Ms Cow was able to perceive that she didn't have much ground to stand on - even allowing for her bulk and weight - in the face of the entire population chanting *We Want Wolf! We Want Wolf!*
She said:
OK, OK, I'll abdicate. But just hang on a mo while I collect my bottles and credit cards.
And without more ado, that was the end of her reign. In case you are interested, she spent the rest of her days on a Hawaiian beach, munching mangos and having guitar lessons, with a saucy bougainvillea tucked behind her ear.

But to return to the moment of her Fall. By now, everyone was in full scale revolt, forgetting that Ms Cow was half way across the Pacific in her private jet. However, kindly, in passing, she had flicked the master switches for all the security codes and locks so, out they all swarmed from the dungeons through the secret trap door; out they poured from the cinemas, campuses, rock concerts and football stadiums where they had been hiding.

Meanwhile, the team of experts and Doctor Pot were still making their researches into the sickness syndrome. They couldn't understand why suddenly their statistics went haywire, and the morgues emptied; even those who did drop dead, promptly recovered and raced off down the village, waving banners and singing, popping balloons and shouting: **Long Live Super-Jo! Super-Jo, the super!** He was their first democratically elected representative after all - *Hurray! Hurray!*

Maybe it is no surprise, but it wasn't long before Super-Jo began to exhibit singularly sinister retrograde traits such as gnawing window-sills, table legs and saucepan handles, as well as tripping up old ladies.

I forgot to mention that by now Hermit had retired. He spent most of his spare time, of which he had oodles since Hetty ran away, communing with Glug. Glug lived in a spooky little hut at the bottom of the forest with her three-legged cat and her three-legged pet frog. Even the downfall of Ms Cow and the shining prospects of Super-Jo's new career could not inveigle Hermit away from his new found soul-mate; in fact, all material matters relating to his erstwhile Alpha status had now become totally meaningless to him - to the extent that one might even justifiably question his proper legal status as **w.o.l.f.** The onus had clearly transmigrated fully and satisfactorily to his off-spring.

Thus my, or rather, *his* tale comes to a close, full spiral, more or less back to the point we started from; though hopefully allowing for an evolutionary mutational shift in so doing - for surely, by now, hadn't everyone come to see that the best thing for the wolf is to be wolfy, and the Others, to be their Others, without discrepancy, exemption or excuse. As Alf Loaf, the village oracle reminded me, before I forgot, that it is only when a cow stops being cowish and a sheep forgets its sheepishness that things really get stuck. As for the rest, those visions of perfect peace and painlessness - who said those could ever be realized without challenge and struggle? No one I know!

MIND-WEAVERS

Mind-weavers!

Purple reminiscences flicker and fold
in old, day-bright ideas.

Then, it was easy.

Happy was a strange, bewitching experience
not a concept, aim or regret.

Somehow

green and buttercup gold
mould and shudder against the eidetic memory wall.

Their tiny detail is distinct

like shreds of morning - youth mornings
spangled with a giddy identification with the populous air.

Then

the mauve, mist-washed sea horizon was an intoxication
a celestial flight into other worlds.

It grows

like straggly wild flowers out of my rainbow skull
and crowns me with a garden of ache-breath joy.

Oh! but it is too lovely

to cramp into syllables and margin-tongued print.
It is too private and beautiful.

It is a vision

That grows like a fairy-weed out of my in-turned eye.
It is alive and lavender blue, like harebells.

Mind-weavers!

THE GENTLEMAN FROM TURKESTAN.

Oh *Mummy*
yelled the wretched toddler Lucy May
he
- that's Henry Will
has broken my doll.

She got up
and looking upon those infants of her prodigy
with severe disenchantment
knocked their heads together without further ado
and at last took the leap, jumping off the ledge
clutching her skirts for decencies sake.

It just so happened
that she landed on a passing open top bus
straight into the lap
of this gentleman from Turkestan.
It doesn't surprise me a bit
she said, straightening her bodice
and consenting to his indecent proposal
forthwith.

THE WIND IN MY TREETOPS

Put the spokes of your wind in my treetops
stiffly, to stir my dry veins.

It is winter in the desert, sand-bright grit
on the surface of my eye.
Creaks back and forth, the old man wind
many sharp-tongued, spiking each root and pore;
stiff and bladed, without any give or softness
hard muscled -and I am only the widow of all seasons.

I am only - only am I.
A puny thing perched on the rim of grammar
speculating about time-machining at the Schwartschild Radius
and if it means God;
or where I may find where I went
- before I did.

Did the thin air ask?
It is winter, remember.
Dry times.
Kites traipse skeins of cloud about the compass:
brittle winds nag at north corners:
flurries of dust unhamper the camels
stalking out of the vanishing point:
Moon, deflowered, hitches itself on the wall
computer footprints on its flanks.

But I am not sour!
Eager are my three eyes for all fickle, risky things.
That is why I like this impersonal, crusty wind
- humourless, in human terms.
But the joke is against us, in fact;
for I see the wind, skirly with laughter
ridiculing our pompous delights.
It dances and scurries in the gutter
skittish with satire!
It tiptoes, tweaking the solemn nose of protocol!
Then, it lies lazy-low
unstirred by animate pain until it rises
rampant, erotic, devastating
pummelling our concrete marvels
into abstracts of warped steel and gently tossing weeds
breeding on bones and pride.

Even a long finger finds its way in here
under the door.
It gets in my lungs, my synthesis
and I find, wind,
you strange, alien thing
- I am the same as you!

PURPLE SWANS

You must be wrong!
for I am positive as I am I
(which perhaps I am not very…)
that today really is today.

Your calendar must be wrong, my friend!
It's years have slipped.
No? well, your eyes?
Optical illusions, then
just like those boomeranging silver darts I saw
reversing in the sky:
or, those purple swans on your suburban lawn, at dusk:
you *saw* them in full flight
- don't you remember?

Today really *is* today!
How can you doubt it?
Are you absolutely *sure*?
Can you prove it?

I have always been one for suspecting the Impossible:
- <u>when</u> it is proved!
But I accept those purple swans
I quite believe you.

I have always been one for doubting
the veracity of our Answers
- let alone the Questions! -
But since you say so
today MUST be today.
Despite my own certainty
that it is something, somewhere else!

I have always been one for suspecting
that differences and opposites
are not necessarily mutually exclusive…
…if we had the eyes!

So you being right
- and me too, relatively
then where is YESTER-day?
A missing spoke in compression vacuum?
A lag, a snaggy, giddy whirl
That caught *me* in its spin?
while *you*, gliding separately
arrive on the spate of the continuum
synchronously!

COMFORTER OF TIME-PASSING

He was old and full of evil:
a cistern of slime.
His greeny, mildewed hair
was the crust of his deeds
grown cold and old.

His mould-effects were a sprouting virus patch.
I prefer to avoid his allotment.
But today, he squats amoebically in front of himself
masticating his rotty gums.
As I thin to pass myself, invisibly
he grabs my manners
and behind his slum-condensed face
I hear him say:
Aha! Got you, juicy fly!
Outside, he translates:
G'mornin' Miss! Fine day an' all.

Sweet-peas are rampant;
he must give me some.
But he will not detain me with his Old Man's chat!
Good-bye! good-bye!

The sweet-peas, like tendrils of bacilli
infect my hand.
My nerve-ends totter and recoil.
When I pass the corner, I fling them in the ditch
where they lie, a flab of abuse
offering themselves cheaply, for a price.

He is old.
Old as innocence - an accumulation.
He is the comforter of time-passing.

OF ADAM, OF EVE

Onceupona
there was a son and daughter
of Adam, of Eve:
the meeting point of their fusion
the fission of their folly.
A genderless biped who bred, spread
like a fungus over the blue planet
until it reached the antipodes of even that most pagan land
where hoard upon hoard of faceless, sex-obsessed creatures
strove in a frenetic search of extinction
thinking that meant Peace - Stillness - non-being.

In that last corner
in an old house
propped on a lollopy bank
at about 4a.m. of a mad full moon
sat Adam, sat Eve
(or their prototypes)
on a rug, playing cards, telling fairy-tales by candlelight
when *suddenly*
- as down the aeons it always was -
the last song hung its last thread
among the moon beamed, cobweb-shadows
and hands fell still…eyes met.

Is that all? - *eyes met?* Pah!
He was leaning, hands trailed
curved, caressing over the music's final creak
while the white light cavorted beyond the dusty window-panes
carrying fairy-kings on unicorns over the mistletoe
and down the hawthorn and oak-splodged lanes.

So he sat
like a cat
hung in a trellis of vain red hair
fey Celtic eyes frozen.
And she, who would have been Genevieve, Delilah
would have embodied all the lascivious graces of her kind
squatted gawky, wilful, zany
eyes frozen too.

O sister, demoness, be mine!
Brother, lover, tongue-tied oracle!
Come! Begone!
I hunger for, I run from you!
In your root I know you - you are mine. . . !

. . . forgetting there was no such thing;
mine, yours, you, me
we belong to no-where, no-one
have played the chattel game
been the real estate - the curse, the crown - in the proprietor's shop;
been trammelled, chained, beholden
made the fidelity trip
true in all but the intent
(who is fooled? who, cuckold?).
Pure as the driven, in my apparent sheet
my record of unsmirched virtuosity
the list of Thou Shalt Nots
still holding fear-born sway
intimidating the timid
-the doubters, the seekers, the lovers, the losers -
so they dare not doubt/seek/lose or love.

64

Ah, but woman groaned he, that First Man
ancient in his new knowledge
but she
enchantress, seductress
no-one could sleep with her!

No sooner is the hard work over
when, what does she do but sit up
and look around for some garment to rend
addressing her God
Oh God! says she
what am I doing here?
and gets out the hoover.

Budge over you lazy sonofabitch
I must vacuum this bed of all its sins
even the horrors in your hair and mind
setting about her expiation
Sleep? Ha!

I will not be one more notch on your cane
One more investment for your pride
One more titivation for your creepy Freudian Id.
I've tried all that
and the keep-me-pure-for-one-and-only
the virgin option of Mr Impossible Right.
I'm not up for lease, rent or sale
not even on a long-term, mutual interest rate
etc. etc.

Whose arguing with you? snored he
from under the quilt.
PS Why don't you go to sleep, you old hag!?

No, but I'm serious.
This is not the time for facetiousness
pulling on gumboots and guilt
I want a home, a man, security.
I want him for myself
who will come to my bed only
even when my skin grows old
and I cannot enwitch him anymore.
Why should I spend my flower
on those who scorn my fading?
"old hag?" Yes! Look!
Wake-up you man-thing, you soporific lump and see!
See these wrinkles in my eye and mind
the way my breasts now sag;
can't you see
when I'm not beautiful
what will you see?
I will not be party to anymore co-operative agreements
between any parties
especially with those I love.
I will not trap us in conditions with safeguarding clauses
and ways to back out.
I will not, on principle agree with or to
anything you propose.
Propose?
I will take thee to me, my welded mate.

What?
How long for?
Tonight? A life or two? A week?
Until you hurt me? Until I am bored? Until the bills come in?

So, skip it!
I will just stare incestuously into thine soul
and there I will see you bare
and every inch explore.
To refuel on the fire of you
Oh my dire flame!

There we will freely meet
on the tip of white-hot desire
the way we fit, rest, complement, interlock, spark off
and wittingly, willingly open up.

That is enough.

CONKER GIRL

Glossy and sleek
conker girl
she has bits of sun-shot hair
straggling in her eyes, bright
with no idea who, how, where she came.
Headlong, quantum-blobbed
her vital ignorance a pestilence, enigma
godsent, presumably.

Knees begin to creak going up the stairs
old conker girl, withered and flabby
dropped breasts and sprogs
multiple mother
skin grown into a shoe.
How *can* the lass
- fresh as jersey cream and dainty -
ever imagine her couteur body-bag
could become such crocodilly footwear?

Yet it is not the years, not time
that stitches these incompatible two
into one continuous conker creature.
One, gallivanting in silly innocence
fresh as a cowpat and ancient in helplessness
was never half as young
as the wizened other
conker oldie, full of softest graces
strengths of the sapling, the lithe wind's breath
like butterfly kisses and quick tongues of flame.
No time-warped, superannuated end-of-the-liner, she.

It is a seamless trick
optically deluded, inside out
paradiza-doxical.
Poor kid, conker babe!

WHOSE WHO

Plumb in the middle of Space
dead centre
there was this Machine
programmed to respond to every imaginable stimulus
- even the *un*imaginable were categorized
as Probabilities!

So
bearing in mind that the space of Space it occupied
was the only part of the whole universe
that it could not <u>see</u>
and that every other vibration would
- at some stage in its trek across eternity -
impinge upon its lenses, pass its scanning eye
what happened then
when that unnatural creature
with his chaotic freewill, turned up!?

"Here I am!" he announced.
then, being inquisitive as well as rash
without more ado
he poked his fingers down the Receptor Valves.

In a nano-second of course
the Machine had it on a plate:
that this was a carbon-atomed living thing
a self-replicating, micro/macro organism
of a certain DNA complexity
with a faculty to correlate, speculate, analogise. . .

Mean-the-while
the carbon-atomed living thing
had pitched his tent under the Particle Relay rim
and struck a match against its side, to light his pipe.
Already, **he** had decided that this object
was not what he was looking for.
It was too solid - with *edges* - to be "God".

Well, the Machine
being an ultra-fictional model
didn't take long to decipher the cerebral gestalt
of this irreverent conglomeration of cells
(whose interlocking systems combined in a synthesis called "I").

But it could not pin down the *source* of its thinking
- what and where it was:
Was there a black hole in its core?
A cog missing?
Where was its initiating "something"?
Its prime impulse?

Even the laws of laterality, of paradox
of statistical chance and abstractness
were inapplicable. . .
. . .proof!

71

Suddenly
the unnatural creature
leapt into the sky with a loud shout
at the precise moment he did
- he had an *I*D*E*A*
viz:
God was <u>behind</u> the Machine
occupying its interior anti-matter.
(for he had searched *every*where else!)

A red light lit up on the Machine's monitor.
It proceeded, according to protocol
to check its *own* circuits.
But all was found in order.

Therefore, it had to be
the carbon-atomed living thing that was at fault.
All other organisms of even remotely similar design
conformed to certain basic structural blueprints
strictured within networks of Causes, Goals, Time or Chemistry
while welded immutably to karmic identities and accounts.

By which time, the offending creature
had got down from the sky
and was sitting cross-kneed, eyeing the Machine askance.
Without preamble, he said:
If you are what you <u>think</u> you are
why, you can self-destruct:
then we'll see whose who!

To which provocation, the Machine
being of exemplary logic
found no reason to respond
especially as it was aware of the creature's *intent!*
It just continued at light-speed sifting the billions of alternatives
to account for that fortuity.

At this rate - it began to deduce
It would require INfinite numbers and possibilities
INfinite resources and perspectives.
And although it was constructed
to be able to face the *theory* of infinity
here it was confronted with the existential *fact*
- albeit disguised behind the façade of indeterminacy
and in the ludicrous skin of mortality.

This it could not countenance.
Thereupon, the whole caboodle
just BLEW UP
into a (finite quanta of) smithereens.

After inspecting the space in which the Machine had been
the carbon-atomed creature was content:
all he found there was a ghost.
Any searching left was inward.

I must be He, he said.

H_2O

The rivers are running dry,
Beetle People.
The Wells are blind,
And the stratosphere
Is schitzoid with drunken fall-out;
But, Beetle People,
I am as thirsty as a carbon atom
And stay alive for years
On blocks of chaff and granite.
The saline earth and evaporated seas
Are kind and comfortable to me.

The rain is turned to falling diamond petals
So even the plebians grow parchment-rich.
Artesian wonders are raped as Neolithic caverns
And I am made of pith, and little humour,
Beetle people.
Blood is rusty powder
And skin is split.

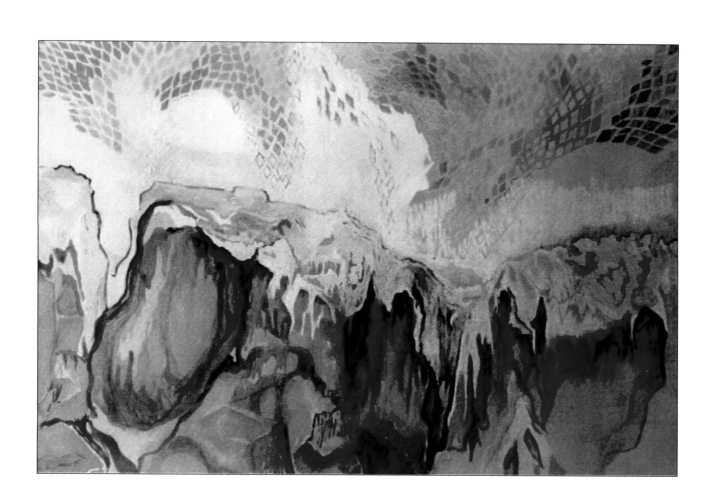

CHILD OF STRAW

Grandmother is a witch
and lives in a corrugated haystack.
Censor the cat
- the cat she belongs to -
terrorizes the gypsy children
with its glare.

That pale blue cup and saucer
she said to me
that hangs in the old yew
belonged to great-Aunt Lucy's Siamese.
Fetch it, child of straw!
I want to make some tea.

There, hanging in the tree by his braces
was the gardener, rotating like a crazy weather-cock
spun slowly, this way and that.
The baling string around his knees
was frayed and like my hair
I thought.

A giant marrow called Gustav
is on the trestle table
where the prize-winning babies are stacked.
Fetch it, daughter of the Muse!
grandmother said.
Censor stalked, fracturing the air.

There, in the candy-floss marquee
sat the vicar like a toadstool:
I, the voice in the wilderness
as he sprinkled the taffeta ladies
with lavender water. . .
. . .but I fled
clutching my pagan-ness to me
- and Censor smiled.

Edward Gaskell *publishers*
DEVON